Student Record Book

MW01153865

SRA Reading LABORATORY® 1a

SRA

Columbus, Ohio

The **McGraw-Hill** Companies

SRAonline.com

 **SRA**

Send all inquiries to:
SRA/McGraw-Hill
4400 Easton Commons
Columbus, Ohio 43219

0-07-602818-6 (Reorder No./Pkg. 5)
R28186.01 (Loose book number)

7 8 9 HSO   13 12 11 10

Contents

Letter to Parents

Over the years, millions of children from cities such as New York, London, Chicago, Toronto, Los Angeles, and Sydney have had one thing in common—they have used "the SRA." "The SRA" is what students have often called *SRA Reading Laboratory.* This school year your child will be using SRA's most recent *Reading Laboratory.* This multileveled system of individualized instruction will provide your child with practice in reading comprehension, vocabulary skills, and study skills. In most classrooms, this program will supplement your child's reader, giving him or her extra reinforcement in a wide range of reading-related skills.

SRA Reading Laboratory offers 144 reading selections. These selections include high-interest nonfiction and fiction that cover a wide range of topics. The settings of many of the stories or articles take place in a variety of places around the world. These selections offer enjoyment in reading for the students, as well as providing them with important information that will broaden their understanding of many global concerns, events, and issues. The reading selections are divided into levels. Each level is represented by a different color, and each color is more difficult to read than the previous color. Therefore, when you hear, "Today I started in Blue!" you are learning of a significant accomplishment.

Each selection is accompanied by exercises that test for students' understanding of the selection. Additional exercises provide practice in vocabulary, word building, and study skills. At the beginning of the school year, each student is placed in a level at which he or she can read successfully. The system then allows your child to move through the levels as fast and as far as his or her ability permits.

Students have been using and enjoying *SRA Reading Laboratory* since 1957. You may have used one of the earlier editions yourself! May your knowledge of this most recent edition increase your understanding of your child's reading enjoyment and progress.

Who Likes to Swim?

by Peter Young

Starter Story

Susan likes to swim, so she went to the pond in the woods. She took her cat, Dippy, along.

Susan jumped in for a swim.

"Come on, Dippy. It's fun." But Dippy just sat on a rock.

Then the rock moved. It was really a turtle. It jumped into the pond, so Dippy had a swim. The turtle liked it, but Dippy did not.

SRA Reading Laboratory 1a

A Read each question. Write *a* or *b*.

1 Why is this story funny?
   a Because Dippy went swimming anyway
   b Because the turtle liked to swim

2 How was Dippy not like Susan?
   a Dippy didn't like turtles.
   b Dippy didn't like to swim.

3 Why did Dippy sit on a rock?
   a So he could get a ride
   b So he would not get wet

4 How were Susan and the turtle the same?
   a They both liked to swim.
   b They both lived at the pond.

5 What was Dippy at the end of the story?
   a He was a wet cat.
   b He was a glad cat.

B s + **ad** = **sad**

Say the word *sad*. Listen to the sound of *ad*. Then look at the letters in the box. Add each letter to *ad* to make a word. Write the word.

1 b	
2 h	+ **ad**
3 d	

C Read the words you wrote. Which one best fits in each sentence? Write the word.

4 Don't feel _____ if you can't swim.

5 Maybe your _____ will show you how.

6 Susan _____ a good time at the pond.

THINK ABOUT IT

D One word in each pair of sentences is underlined. Find the opposite of the underlined word in the other sentence. Write the word.

1 It was a <u>hot</u> day.
   The water in the pond was cold.

2 The turtle had a <u>hard</u> shell.
   Dippy had soft fur.

3 Susan could swim a <u>long</u> way.
   The turtle had a short tail.

4 Dippy jumped <u>up</u> in the air.
   Susan went down into the water.

Starter Story Record Page

Name _____ Date _____

Power Builder Color _____ Power Builder Number _____

A Comprehension

1 _____ 2 _____ 3 _____ 4 _____ 5 _____

Number Correct [ ]

B, C Learn about Words

1 _____ 6 _____

2 _____ 7 _____

3 _____ 8 _____

4 _____ 9 _____

5 _____ 10 _____

Number Correct [ ]

Think about It

D 1 _____ **E** 6 _____

2 _____ 7 _____

3 _____ 8 _____

4 _____ 9 _____

5 _____ 10 _____

Number Correct [ ]

Where Was the Bird?

by Carolyn Larsen

Conner was in a pet shop. He was looking at the pets. Then a bird got out of its cage.

Other people were in the shop with Conner. Mrs. Olsen looked at the cats. Rosario watched the fish. But nobody saw the bird. Where was it?

Then Mrs. Olsen left the shop. The bird got away. It left on Mrs. Olsen's hat.

SRA Reading Laboratory 1a

A Read each question. Write *a* or *b.*

1 What is another good name for this story?
a Conner Gets a Pet
b Out on a Hat

2 Why didn't Rosario see the bird?
a Because she was in another room
b Because she was looking at the fish

3 Why was the bird hard to see?
a Because it looked like Mrs. Olsen's hat
b Because it was behind the pet shop door

4 Why did Mrs. Olsen go to the pet shop?
a To look at the cats
b To get a bird

5 What did Mrs. Olsen have when she came out of the pet shop?
a A cat
b A bird

B w + **et** = **wet**

Say the word *wet.* Listen to the sound of *et.* Then look at the letters in the box. Add each letter to *et* to make a word. Write the word.

> 1 l
> 2 p + **et**
> 3 g

C Read the words you wrote. Which one best fits in each sentence? Write the word.

4 Conner was looking in a _____ shop.
5 Who _____ the bird out of its cage?
6 Nobody saw the bird _____ away.

D Read each sentence. Look at the <u>underlined</u> word. Find the word in the box that means almost the same thing. Write the word.

> glad   shop   hat   small

1 The pet <u>store</u> was full of animals.
2 The bird was <u>little</u>.
3 The bird sat on Mrs. Olsen's <u>cap</u>.
4 The bird was <u>happy</u> to be out of its cage.

Starter Story Record Page

Name _____   Date _____

Power Builder Color _____   Power Builder Number _____

A Comprehension

1 _____   2 _____   3 _____   4 _____   5 _____

Number Correct [   ]

B, C Learn about Words

1 _____   6 _____

2 _____   7 _____

3 _____   8 _____

4 _____   9 _____

5 _____   10 _____

Number Correct [   ]

Think about It

D 1 _____   **E** 6 _____

2 _____   7 _____

3 _____   8 _____

4 _____   9 _____

5 _____   10 _____

Number Correct [   ]

At the Bus Stop

by Judy Scroggin

Rose 1a
Starter Story

Samantha watches the people at the bus stop. They are going to work. The bus comes. They get on. Then the bus leaves.

Samantha does not get on that bus. But sometimes she wishes she did. It could be fun to work.

Then the school bus comes. Samantha gets on. Her friends are there. She's happy. Another school day begins.

SRA Reading Laboratory 1a

A Read each question. Write *a* or *b.*

1 What makes Samantha glad in this story?
   a The fun she has at work
   b The friends on her bus

2 When were the people getting on the bus?
   a They were getting on in the morning.
   b They were getting on at night.

3 Why didn't Samantha get on the first bus?
   a There wasn't room for her.
   b It wasn't a school bus.

4 Why did Samantha sometimes want to ride the first bus?
   a Because she wanted to try going to work
   b Because she wanted to miss school

5 How was Samantha like the people at the bus stop?
   a They all rode buses.
   b They all went to work.

B s + **ay** = **say**

Say the word *say.* Listen to the sound of *ay.* Then look at the letters in the box. Add each letter to *ay* to make a word. Write the word.

1	d
2	m + **ay**
3	w

C Read the words you wrote. Which one best fits in each sentence? Write the word.

4 Samantha is on her _____ to school.

5 The bus _____ be late.

6 Soon the school _____ will be over.

D Here are some sentences about buses. If the sentence tells why people ride buses, write *yes.* If it does not tell why people ride buses, write *no.*

1 A bus takes people to work.

2 A school bus takes up a lot of room.

3 A school bus takes children to school.

4 A bus takes people home.

Starter Story Record Page

Name _____   Date _____

Power Builder Color _____   Power Builder Number _____

A Comprehension

1 _____   2 _____   3 _____   4 _____   5 _____

Number Correct [   ]

B, C Learn about Words

1 _____   6 _____

2 _____   7 _____

3 _____   8 _____

4 _____   9 _____

5 _____   10 _____

Number Correct [   ]

Think about It

D 1 _____   E 6 _____

2 _____   7 _____

3 _____   8 _____

4 _____   9 _____

5 _____   10 _____

Number Correct [   ]

21

First Place

by John Wickes

Cassie saw a sign in a shop. It read, "Big Race Today."

"I know I can win," Cassie said.

Cassie's dad drove her to the park. The race began. Cassie ran as fast as she could. But she came in last. Cassie was very sad.

Then her dad drove her to an ice-cream shop. He said, "You'll always be a winner to me."

Cassie smiled and ate her ice cream. There would be a next time.

SRA Reading Laboratory 1a

A Read each question. Write *a* or *b*.

1 What is another good name for this story?
a A Winner to Dad
b A Day at the Park

2 Why wasn't Cassie happy at the end of the race?
a She ran fast, but she didn't win.
b She knew her dad wanted her to win.

3 What did Cassie's dad want?
a He wanted to make Cassie happy.
b He wanted Cassie to win the next race.

4 What will Cassie most likely do in the next race?
a She will not try hard.
b She will try to win.

5 What will Cassie's dad most likely do before Cassie's next race?
a He will give her ice cream again.
b He will tell her to try her best.

B p + **an** = **pan**

Say the word *pan.* Listen to the sound of *an.* Then look at the letters in the box. Add each letter to *an* to make a word. Write the word.

1 c	
2 m	+ **an**
3 r	

C Read the words you wrote. Which one best fits in each sentence? Write the word.

4 A _____ put a sign in his shop.

5 Cassie said, "I _____ win this race!"

6 Cassie _____ as fast as she could.

D *Mouse* and *house* end the same way. They rhyme. Write the word that ends like or rhymes with the underlined word.

1 Cassie wanted to <u>win</u>.
   She could not wait to (begin, end).

2 Cassie tried to run <u>fast</u>.
   Cassie came in (first, last).

3 The race made Cassie feel <u>sad</u>.
   She had ice cream with her (dad, father).

4 She might win the next <u>race</u>.
   Then she will have a smile on her (face, lips).

Starter Story Record Page

Name _____ Date _____

Power Builder Color _____ Power Builder Number _____

A Comprehension

1 _____ 2 _____ 3 _____ 4 _____ 5 _____

Number Correct [ ]

B, C Learn about Words

1 _____ 6 _____

2 _____ 7 _____

3 _____ 8 _____

4 _____ 9 _____

5 _____ 10 _____

Number Correct [ ]

Think about It

D 1 _____ **E** 6 _____

2 _____ 7 _____

3 _____ 8 _____

4 _____ 9 _____

5 _____ 10 _____

Number Correct [ ]

DOG OVERBOARD!

by Dan Browning

Bernard was crossing the sea by ship. He liked to nap. Bernard had a dog named Mutton. He napped on the ship with Bernard.

One day, Mutton woke up. Then he fell overboard!

"Stop the ship!" Bernard shouted. "Mutton will drown! Save him!"

The captain came. "I'm sorry, sir. I can't stop the ship for a dog. It's against the rules. I can only stop the ship if a person is drowning."

"Very well," said Bernard. Then he jumped into the sea.

"Stop the ship!" shouted the captain. Nobody saw Bernard's lifejacket!

They stopped the ship. Bernard got on it. The captain saved Mutton. Then Bernard and Mutton took a nap.

A Read each question. Write *a* or *b*.

1 What is this story about?
   a Knowing how to save a person
   b Finding a way to help others

2 When Mutton fell overboard, where did he go?
   a He fell into the water.
   b He fell over a board.

3 Why did Bernard jump off the ship?
   a Because he wanted to save Mutton
   b Because he wanted to swim with Mutton

4 Why did the captain stop the ship?
   a To get Bernard out of the water
   b To get Mutton out of the water

5 What will Bernard most likely do next?
   a Thank the captain for going against the rules
   b Thank the captain for saving Mutton

LEARN ABOUT WORDS

B w + **ay** = **way**

Say the word *way.* Listen to the sound of *ay.* Then look at the letters in the box. Add each letter or group of letters to *ay* to make a word. Write the word.

1 p	
2 m	
3 pl + **ay**	
4 st	
5 tr	

⟶

LEARN ABOUT WORDS

C Read the words you wrote. Which one best fits in each sentence? Write the word.

6 Bernard's dog liked to _____ with a ball.

7 The dog knocked over a _____ of food.

8 Bernard had to _____ a lot of money for the food.

9 The dog had to _____ home after that.

10 Bernard _____ not take another boat trip.

THINK ABOUT IT

D Look at each picture. Answer the questions. Write *a* or *b.*

1 What will the man do next?
  a Go into the water
  b Go back home

2 How do you know?
  a He is tired and ready to leave.
  b He is at a swimming pool.

3 What will the woman do next?
  a Cook a fish
  b Catch a fish

4 How do you know?
  a She is fishing.
  b She is hungry.

Starter Story Record Page

Name _____ Date _____

Power Builder Color _____ Power Builder Number _____

A Comprehension

1 _____ 2 _____ 3 _____ 4 _____ 5 _____

Number Correct [   ]

B, C Learn about Words

1 _____ 6 _____

2 _____ 7 _____

3 _____ 8 _____

4 _____ 9 _____

5 _____ 10 _____

Number Correct [   ]

Think about It

D1 _____ E6 _____

2 _____ 7 _____

3 _____ 8 _____

4 _____ 9 _____

5 _____ 10 _____

Number Correct [   ]

The Space Suit

by Bettye Jenkins

Dave's class was having a costume party. All the students in his class came to school in costume.

Jordan came dressed as a blue whale. Pedro came dressed as a hairy ape. Missy was a white rabbit. Pam was a colorful bird.

Dave got to school last. He did not wear a fancy costume like his friends. He was wearing his father's old suit. It was much too big for Dave.

"What are you?" asked Jordan.

"He's a man in a baggy suit," said Pedro.

"No," said Dave. "I'm an astronaut."

"An astronaut wears a space suit!" said Pam. "You're not wearing a space suit."

"Yes, I am," said Dave. "There's enough space in this suit for three of me!"

A Read each question. Write *a* or *b*.

1 What is funny in this story?
    a The word *space* names two things.
    b Dave's father was an astronaut.

2 Why was Dave most likely the last one to school?
    a Because he was reading about space suits
    b Because he was putting on his costume

3 Why did Dave have on his father's suit?
    a Because it was his costume
    b Because his father told him to wear it

4 How was Pam's costume not like Dave's costume?
    a Pam's costume was big and funny.
    b Pam's costume wasn't hard to guess.

5 Why didn't people know what Dave's costume was?
    a They didn't know what a space suit looked like.
    b They didn't know Dave was playing a trick.

B h + **all** = **hall**

Say the word *hall*. Listen to the sound of *all*. Then look at the letters in the box. Add each letter or group of letters to *all* to make a word. Write the word.

1 c	
2 f	
3 t	+ **all**
4 sm	
5 w	

C Read the words you wrote. Which one best fits in each sentence? Write the word.

    6 Dave's father is six feet _____.

    7 Dave is too _____ for his dad's suit.

    8 The pants might even _____ down.

    9 Dave likes to _____ his costume a space suit.

  10 His teacher put a picture of Dave on the _____.

D Read each pair of words. Write the word that comes first in alphabetical order.

    1 sheet   class

    2 big   fancy

    3 school   daddy

    4 whale   space

Starter Story Record Page

Name _____ Date _____

Power Builder Color _____ Power Builder Number _____

A Comprehension

1 _____ 2 _____ 3 _____ 4 _____ 5 _____

Number Correct [   ]

B, C Learn about Words

1 _____ 6 _____

2 _____ 7 _____

3 _____ 8 _____

4 _____ 9 _____

5 _____ 10 _____

Number Correct [   ]

Think about It

D 1 _____ **E** 6 _____

2 _____ 7 _____

3 _____ 8 _____

4 _____ 9 _____

5 _____ 10 _____

Number Correct [   ]

Get Ready to Read . . .

When you read a story, you read sentences that belong together. They all help to tell about one **main idea.** The main idea is what the story is mostly about. Clues about the main idea will help you understand what you read. Here are some things to look for.

What Do You See?

You can use your eyes to get clues about the main idea of a story.

● **Look at the picture.** ·

● **Read the title.** ·

● **Read the first sentence.** ·

● **Read the last paragraph.** ·

All these clues will help you find the story's main idea.

Pat's Balloon

Pat had a balloon. She put her name on the balloon. Then, she let it go up in the air. "I hope a boy or girl finds my balloon," she said.

A boy named Don did find Pat's balloon. He read Pat's name. "I know that girl!" he said. Don went to Pat's house. Pat was surprised to see her balloon again.

Strategy Lesson 2

As You Read...

It is important to keep asking yourself questions as you read. This will help you understand what you read even better and enjoy it more.

What Do You Think?

Now, read the story "Pat's Balloon" and ask yourself these questions:

- **Did I guess what the story is mostly about?**

- **Do I understand what I just read in this paragraph?**

- **What did I learn from this story?**

These questions will help you get the most out of what you read.

Pat's Balloon

Pat had a balloon. She put her name on the balloon. Then, she let it go up in the air. "I hope a boy or girl finds my balloon," she said.

A boy named Don did find Pat's balloon. He read Pat's name. "I know that girl!" he said. Don went to Pat's house. Pat was surprised to see her balloon again.

After You Read . . .

After you read a story, you usually know more than you did before. There are many ways to find out how well you understood what you read. One simple way is to answer questions.

What Do You Know?

Answer the questions below. Turn back to the story if you need help.

1 Pat put her name on
   a a tree.
   b the balloon.

2 The boy who found the balloon was
   a Don.
   b Pat.

3 The main idea is
   a Pat is surprised when her balloon comes back.
   b Don is surprised when he finds the balloon.

4 Another good title for this story is
   a Pat's Big Surprise.
   b Pat and Don Are Friends.

Go to page 128 in this book to check your answers.

Keep in Mind . . .

Before You Read

Use your eyes to get clues about the main idea:

- Look at the picture.

- Read the title.

- Read the first sentence.

- Read the last paragraph.

As You Read

Ask yourself these questions as you read to make sure you understand:

- Did I guess what the story is mostly about?

- Do I understand what I just read?

- What did I learn from this story?

Record Page

Name _____ Date _____

Power Builder Color _____ Power Builder Number _____

A Comprehension

1 _____ 2 _____ 3 _____ 4 _____ 5 _____

Number Correct [   ]

B, C Learn about Words

1 _____ 6 _____

2 _____ 7 _____

3 _____ 8 _____

4 _____ 9 _____

5 _____ 10 _____

Number Correct [   ]

Think about It

D 1 _____ **E** 6 _____

2 _____ 7 _____

3 _____ 8 _____

4 _____ 9 _____

5 _____ 10 _____

Number Correct [   ]

Record Page

Name _____ Date _____

Power Builder Color _____ Power Builder Number _____

A Comprehension

1 _____ 2 _____ 3 _____ 4 _____ 5 _____

Number Correct [   ]

B, C Learn about Words

1 _____ 6 _____

2 _____ 7 _____

3 _____ 8 _____

4 _____ 9 _____

5 _____ 10 _____

Number Correct [   ]

Think about It

D 1 _____ **E** 6 _____

2 _____ 7 _____

3 _____ 8 _____

4 _____ 9 _____

5 _____ 10 _____

Number Correct [   ]

Record Page

Name _____ Date _____

Power Builder Color _____ Power Builder Number _____

A Comprehension

1 _____ 2 _____ 3 _____ 4 _____ 5 _____

Number Correct ☐

B, C Learn about Words

1 _____ 6 _____

2 _____ 7 _____

3 _____ 8 _____

4 _____ 9 _____

5 _____ 10 _____

Number Correct ☐

Think about It

D 1 _____ **E** 6 _____

2 _____ 7 _____

3 _____ 8 _____

4 _____ 9 _____

5 _____ 10 _____

Number Correct ☐

Record Page

Name _____ Date _____

Power Builder Color _____ Power Builder Number _____

A Comprehension

1 _____ 2 _____ 3 _____ 4 _____ 5 _____

Number Correct [   ]

B, C Learn about Words

1 _____ 6 _____

2 _____ 7 _____

3 _____ 8 _____

4 _____ 9 _____

5 _____ 10 _____

Number Correct [   ]

Think about It

D 1 _____ E 6 _____

2 _____ 7 _____

3 _____ 8 _____

4 _____ 9 _____

5 _____ 10 _____

Number Correct [   ]

Record Page

Name _____   Date _____

Power Builder Color _____   Power Builder Number _____

A Comprehension

1 _____ 2 _____ 3 _____ 4 _____ 5 _____

Number Correct ☐

B, C Learn about Words

1 _____   6 _____

2 _____   7 _____

3 _____   8 _____

4 _____   9 _____

5 _____   10 _____

Number Correct ☐

Think about It

D 1 _____   **E** 6 _____

2 _____   7 _____

3 _____   8 _____

4 _____   9 _____

5 _____   10 _____

Number Correct ☐

Record Page

Name _____ Date _____

Power Builder Color _____ Power Builder Number _____

A Comprehension

1 _____   2 _____   3 _____   4 _____   5 _____

Number Correct [ ]

B, C Learn about Words

1 _____   6 _____

2 _____   7 _____

3 _____   8 _____

4 _____   9 _____

5 _____   10 _____

Number Correct [ ]

Think about It

D 1 _____   **E** 6 _____

2 _____   7 _____

3 _____   8 _____

4 _____   9 _____

5 _____   10 _____

Number Correct [ ]

Record Page

Name _____ Date _____

Power Builder Color _____ Power Builder Number _____

A Comprehension

1 _____ 2 _____ 3 _____ 4 _____ 5 _____

Number Correct [ ]

B, C Learn about Words

1 _____ 6 _____

2 _____ 7 _____

3 _____ 8 _____

4 _____ 9 _____

5 _____ 10 _____

Number Correct [ ]

Think about It

D1 _____ E6 _____

2 _____ 7 _____

3 _____ 8 _____

4 _____ 9 _____

5 _____ 10 _____

Number Correct [ ]

Record Page

Name _____ Date _____

Power Builder Color _____ Power Builder Number _____

A Comprehension

1 _____ 2 _____ 3 _____ 4 _____ 5 _____

Number Correct ☐

B, C Learn about Words

1 _____ 6 _____

2 _____ 7 _____

3 _____ 8 _____

4 _____ 9 _____

5 _____ 10 _____

Number Correct ☐

Think about It

D 1 _____ **E** 6 _____

2 _____ 7 _____

3 _____ 8 _____

4 _____ 9 _____

5 _____ 10 _____

Number Correct ☐

Record Page

Name _____ Date _____

Power Builder Color _____ Power Builder Number _____

A Comprehension

1 _____ 2 _____ 3 _____ 4 _____ 5 _____

Number Correct ☐

B, C Learn about Words

1 _____ 6 _____

2 _____ 7 _____

3 _____ 8 _____

4 _____ 9 _____

5 _____ 10 _____

Number Correct ☐

Think about It

D1 _____ **E**6 _____

2 _____ 7 _____

3 _____ 8 _____

4 _____ 9 _____

5 _____ 10 _____

Number Correct ☐

Record Page

Name _____   Date _____

Power Builder Color _____   Power Builder Number _____

A Comprehension

1 _____ 2 _____ 3 _____ 4 _____ 5 _____

Number Correct [   ]

B, C Learn about Words

1 _____   6 _____

2 _____   7 _____

3 _____   8 _____

4 _____   9 _____

5 _____   10 _____

Number Correct [   ]

Think about It

D1 _____   **E**6 _____

2 _____   7 _____

3 _____   8 _____

4 _____   9 _____

5 _____   10 _____

Number Correct [   ]

Record Page

Name _____ Date _____

Power Builder Color _____ Power Builder Number _____

A Comprehension

1 _____ 2 _____ 3 _____ 4 _____ 5 _____

Number Correct [ ]

B, C Learn about Words

1 _____ 6 _____

2 _____ 7 _____

3 _____ 8 _____

4 _____ 9 _____

5 _____ 10 _____

Number Correct [ ]

Think about It

D 1 _____ **E** 6 _____

2 _____ 7 _____

3 _____ 8 _____

4 _____ 9 _____

5 _____ 10 _____

Number Correct [ ]

Record Page

Name _____ Date _____

Power Builder Color _____ Power Builder Number _____

A Comprehension

1 _____   2 _____   3 _____   4 _____   5 _____

Number Correct ☐

B, C Learn about Words

1 _____   6 _____

2 _____   7 _____

3 _____   8 _____

4 _____   9 _____

5 _____   10 _____

Number Correct ☐

Think about It

D 1 _____   E 6 _____

2 _____   7 _____

3 _____   8 _____

4 _____   9 _____

5 _____   10 _____

Number Correct ☐

Record Page

Name _____   Date _____

Power Builder Color _____   Power Builder Number _____

A Comprehension

1 _____   2 _____   3 _____   4 _____   5 _____

Number Correct [   ]

B, C Learn about Words

1 _____   6 _____

2 _____   7 _____

3 _____   8 _____

4 _____   9 _____

5 _____   10 _____

Number Correct [   ]

Think about It

D 1 _____   **E** 6 _____

2 _____   7 _____

3 _____   8 _____

4 _____   9 _____

5 _____   10 _____

Number Correct [   ]

Record Page

Name _____ Date _____

Power Builder Color _____ Power Builder Number _____

A Comprehension

1 _____ 2 _____ 3 _____ 4 _____ 5 _____

Number Correct [   ]

B, C Learn about Words

1 _____ 6 _____

2 _____ 7 _____

3 _____ 8 _____

4 _____ 9 _____

5 _____ 10 _____

Number Correct [   ]

Think about It

D 1 _____ **E** 6 _____

2 _____ 7 _____

3 _____ 8 _____

4 _____ 9 _____

5 _____ 10 _____

Number Correct [   ]

Record Page

Name _____ Date _____

Power Builder Color _____ Power Builder Number _____

A Comprehension

1 _____ 2 _____ 3 _____ 4 _____ 5 _____

Number Correct [____]

B, C Learn about Words

1 _____ 6 _____

2 _____ 7 _____

3 _____ 8 _____

4 _____ 9 _____

5 _____ 10 _____

Number Correct [____]

Think about It

D 1 _____ **E** 6 _____

2 _____ 7 _____

3 _____ 8 _____

4 _____ 9 _____

5 _____ 10 _____

Number Correct [____]

Record Page

Name _____   Date _____

Power Builder Color _____   Power Builder Number _____

A Comprehension

1 _____   2 _____   3 _____   4 _____   5 _____

Number Correct [ ]

B, C Learn about Words

1 _____   6 _____

2 _____   7 _____

3 _____   8 _____

4 _____   9 _____

5 _____   10 _____

Number Correct [ ]

Think about It

D 1 _____   **E** 6 _____

2 _____   7 _____

3 _____   8 _____

4 _____   9 _____

5 _____   10 _____

Number Correct [ ]

Record Page

Name _____ Date _____

Power Builder Color _____ Power Builder Number _____

A Comprehension

1 _____ 2 _____ 3 _____ 4 _____ 5 _____

Number Correct [   ]

B, C Learn about Words

1 _____   6 _____

2 _____   7 _____

3 _____   8 _____

4 _____   9 _____

5 _____   10 _____

Number Correct [   ]

Think about It

D1 _____   **E**6 _____

2 _____   7 _____

3 _____   8 _____

4 _____   9 _____

5 _____   10 _____

Number Correct [   ]

Record Page

Name _____ Date _____

Power Builder Color _____ Power Builder Number _____

A Comprehension

1 _____   2 _____   3 _____   4 _____   5 _____

Number Correct ☐

B, C Learn about Words

1 _____   6 _____

2 _____   7 _____

3 _____   8 _____

4 _____   9 _____

5 _____   10 _____

Number Correct ☐

Think about It

D 1 _____   **E** 6 _____

2 _____   7 _____

3 _____   8 _____

4 _____   9 _____

5 _____   10 _____

Number Correct ☐

Record Page

Name _____   Date _____

Power Builder Color _____   Power Builder Number _____

A Comprehension

1 _____   2 _____   3 _____   4 _____   5 _____

Number Correct ☐

B, C Learn about Words

1 _____   6 _____

2 _____   7 _____

3 _____   8 _____

4 _____   9 _____

5 _____   10 _____

Number Correct ☐

Think about It

D 1 _____   **E** 6 _____

2 _____   7 _____

3 _____   8 _____

4 _____   9 _____

5 _____   10 _____

Number Correct ☐

Record Page

Name _____

Date _____

Power Builder Color _____

Power Builder Number _____

A Comprehension

1 _____ 2 _____ 3 _____ 4 _____ 5 _____

Number Correct ☐

B, C Learn about Words

1 _____ 6 _____

2 _____ 7 _____

3 _____ 8 _____

4 _____ 9 _____

5 _____ 10 _____

Number Correct ☐

Think about It

D 1 _____ **E** 6 _____

2 _____ 7 _____

3 _____ 8 _____

4 _____ 9 _____

5 _____ 10 _____

Number Correct ☐

Record Page

Name _____

Date _____

Power Builder Color _____

Power Builder Number _____

A Comprehension

1 _____ 2 _____ 3 _____ 4 _____ 5 _____

Number Correct [   ]

B, C Learn about Words

1 _____

2 _____

3 _____

4 _____

5 _____

6 _____

7 _____

8 _____

9 _____

10 _____

Number Correct [   ]

Think about It

D 1 _____

2 _____

3 _____

4 _____

5 _____

E 6 _____

7 _____

8 _____

9 _____

10 _____

Number Correct [   ]

Record Page

Name _____ Date _____

Power Builder Color _____ Power Builder Number _____

A Comprehension

1 _____ 2 _____ 3 _____ 4 _____ 5 _____

Number Correct [ ]

B, C Learn about Words

1 _____ 6 _____

2 _____ 7 _____

3 _____ 8 _____

4 _____ 9 _____

5 _____ 10 _____

Number Correct [ ]

Think about It

D 1 _____ **E** 6 _____

2 _____ 7 _____

3 _____ 8 _____

4 _____ 9 _____

5 _____ 10 _____

Number Correct [ ]

Record Page

Name _____ Date _____

Power Builder Color _____ Power Builder Number _____

A Comprehension

1 _____ 2 _____ 3 _____ 4 _____ 5 _____

Number Correct [ ]

B, C Learn about Words

1 _____ 6 _____

2 _____ 7 _____

3 _____ 8 _____

4 _____ 9 _____

5 _____ 10 _____

Number Correct [ ]

Think about It

D 1 _____ **E** 6 _____

2 _____ 7 _____

3 _____ 8 _____

4 _____ 9 _____

5 _____ 10 _____

Number Correct [ ]

Record Page

Name _____   Date _____

Power Builder Color _____   Power Builder Number _____

A Comprehension

1 _____ 2 _____ 3 _____ 4 _____ 5 _____

Number Correct [ ]

B, C Learn about Words

1 _____   6 _____

2 _____   7 _____

3 _____   8 _____

4 _____   9 _____

5 _____   10 _____

Number Correct [ ]

Think about It

D 1 _____   **E** 6 _____

2 _____   7 _____

3 _____   8 _____

4 _____   9 _____

5 _____   10 _____

Number Correct [ ]

Record Page

Name _____   Date _____

Power Builder Color _____   Power Builder Number _____

A Comprehension

1 _____   2 _____   3 _____   4 _____   5 _____

Number Correct [   ]

B, C Learn about Words

1 _____   6 _____

2 _____   7 _____

3 _____   8 _____

4 _____   9 _____

5 _____   10 _____

Number Correct [   ]

Think about It

D 1 _____   **E** 6 _____

2 _____   7 _____

3 _____   8 _____

4 _____   9 _____

5 _____   10 _____

Number Correct [   ]

Record Page

Name _____ Date _____

Power Builder Color _____ Power Builder Number _____

A Comprehension

1 _____ 2 _____ 3 _____ 4 _____ 5 _____

Number Correct ☐

B, C Learn about Words

1 _____ 6 _____

2 _____ 7 _____

3 _____ 8 _____

4 _____ 9 _____

5 _____ 10 _____

Number Correct ☐

Think about It

D 1 _____ **E** 6 _____

2 _____ 7 _____

3 _____ 8 _____

4 _____ 9 _____

5 _____ 10 _____

Number Correct ☐

Record Page

Name _____ Date _____

Power Builder Color _____ Power Builder Number _____

A Comprehension

1 _____ 2 _____ 3 _____ 4 _____ 5 _____

Number Correct [ ]

B, C Learn about Words

1 _____ 6 _____

2 _____ 7 _____

3 _____ 8 _____

4 _____ 9 _____

5 _____ 10 _____

Number Correct [ ]

Think about It

D 1 _____ **E** 6 _____

2 _____ 7 _____

3 _____ 8 _____

4 _____ 9 _____

5 _____ 10 _____

Number Correct [ ]

Record Page

Name _____   Date _____

Power Builder Color _____   Power Builder Number _____

A Comprehension

1 _____   2 _____   3 _____   4 _____   5 _____

Number Correct [   ]

B, C Learn about Words

1 _____   6 _____

2 _____   7 _____

3 _____   8 _____

4 _____   9 _____

5 _____   10 _____

Number Correct [   ]

Think about It

D 1 _____   **E** 6 _____

2 _____   7 _____

3 _____   8 _____

4 _____   9 _____

5 _____   10 _____

Number Correct [   ]

Record Page

Name _____ Date _____

Power Builder Color _____ Power Builder Number _____

A Comprehension

1 _____ 2 _____ 3 _____ 4 _____ 5 _____

Number Correct [ ]

B, C Learn about Words

1 _____ 6 _____

2 _____ 7 _____

3 _____ 8 _____

4 _____ 9 _____

5 _____ 10 _____

Number Correct [ ]

Think about It

D1 _____ **E**6 _____

2 _____ 7 _____

3 _____ 8 _____

4 _____ 9 _____

5 _____ 10 _____

Number Correct [ ]

Record Page

Name _____   Date _____

Power Builder Color _____   Power Builder Number _____

A Comprehension

1 _____   2 _____   3 _____   4 _____   5 _____

Number Correct [   ]

B, C Learn about Words

1 _____   6 _____

2 _____   7 _____

3 _____   8 _____

4 _____   9 _____

5 _____   10 _____

Number Correct [   ]

Think about It

D 1 _____   E 6 _____

2 _____   7 _____

3 _____   8 _____

4 _____   9 _____

5 _____   10 _____

Number Correct [   ]

Record Page

Name _____ Date _____

Power Builder Color _____ Power Builder Number _____

A Comprehension

1 _____ 2 _____ 3 _____ 4 _____ 5 _____

Number Correct [____]

B, C Learn about Words

1 _____   6 _____

2 _____   7 _____

3 _____   8 _____

4 _____   9 _____

5 _____   10 _____

Number Correct [____]

Think about It

D 1 _____   **E** 6 _____

2 _____   7 _____

3 _____   8 _____

4 _____   9 _____

5 _____   10 _____

Number Correct [____]

Record Page

Name _____ Date _____

Power Builder Color _____ Power Builder Number _____

A Comprehension

1 _____ 2 _____ 3 _____ 4 _____ 5 _____

Number Correct [ ]

B, C Learn about Words

1 _____ 6 _____

2 _____ 7 _____

3 _____ 8 _____

4 _____ 9 _____

5 _____ 10 _____

Number Correct [ ]

Think about It

D 1 _____ **E** 6 _____

2 _____ 7 _____

3 _____ 8 _____

4 _____ 9 _____

5 _____ 10 _____

Number Correct [ ]

Record Page

Name _____ Date _____

Power Builder Color _____ Power Builder Number _____

A Comprehension

1 _____ 2 _____ 3 _____ 4 _____ 5 _____

Number Correct ☐

B, C Learn about Words

1 _____ 6 _____

2 _____ 7 _____

3 _____ 8 _____

4 _____ 9 _____

5 _____ 10 _____

Number Correct ☐

Think about It

D 1 _____ **E** 6 _____

2 _____ 7 _____

3 _____ 8 _____

4 _____ 9 _____

5 _____ 10 _____

Number Correct ☐

Record Page

Name _____ Date _____

Power Builder Color _____ Power Builder Number _____

A Comprehension

1 _____ 2 _____ 3 _____ 4 _____ 5 _____

Number Correct [   ]

B, C Learn about Words

1 _____ 6 _____

2 _____ 7 _____

3 _____ 8 _____

4 _____ 9 _____

5 _____ 10 _____

Number Correct [   ]

Think about It

D 1 _____ E 6 _____

2 _____ 7 _____

3 _____ 8 _____

4 _____ 9 _____

5 _____ 10 _____

Number Correct [   ]

Record Page

Name _____ Date _____

Power Builder Color _____ Power Builder Number _____

A Comprehension

1 _____ 2 _____ 3 _____ 4 _____ 5 _____

Number Correct [ ]

B, C Learn about Words

1 _____   6 _____

2 _____   7 _____

3 _____   8 _____

4 _____   9 _____

5 _____   10 _____

Number Correct [ ]

Think about It

D 1 _____   **E** 6 _____

2 _____   7 _____

3 _____   8 _____

4 _____   9 _____

5 _____   10 _____

Number Correct [ ]

Record Page

Name _____   Date _____

Power Builder Color _____   Power Builder Number _____

A Comprehension

1 _____   2 _____   3 _____   4 _____   5 _____

Number Correct ☐

B, C Learn about Words

1 _____   6 _____

2 _____   7 _____

3 _____   8 _____

4 _____   9 _____

5 _____   10 _____

Number Correct ☐

Think about It

D 1 _____   **E** 6 _____

2 _____   7 _____

3 _____   8 _____

4 _____   9 _____

5 _____   10 _____

Number Correct ☐

Record Page

Name _____ Date _____

Power Builder Color _____ Power Builder Number _____

A Comprehension

1 _____ 2 _____ 3 _____ 4 _____ 5 _____

Number Correct ☐

B, C Learn about Words

1 _____ 6 _____

2 _____ 7 _____

3 _____ 8 _____

4 _____ 9 _____

5 _____ 10 _____

Number Correct ☐

Think about It

D 1 _____ E 6 _____

2 _____ 7 _____

3 _____ 8 _____

4 _____ 9 _____

5 _____ 10 _____

Number Correct ☐

Record Page

Name _____   Date _____

Power Builder Color _____   Power Builder Number _____

A Comprehension

1 _____   2 _____   3 _____   4 _____   5 _____

Number Correct [ ]

B, C Learn about Words

1 _____   6 _____

2 _____   7 _____

3 _____   8 _____

4 _____   9 _____

5 _____   10 _____

Number Correct [ ]

Think about It

D 1 _____   **E** 6 _____

2 _____   7 _____

3 _____   8 _____

4 _____   9 _____

5 _____   10 _____

Number Correct [ ]

Record Page

Name _____   Date _____

Power Builder Color _____   Power Builder Number _____

A Comprehension

1 _____   2 _____   3 _____   4 _____   5 _____

Number Correct [   ]

B, C Learn about Words

1 _____   6 _____

2 _____   7 _____

3 _____   8 _____

4 _____   9 _____

5 _____   10 _____

Number Correct [   ]

Think about It

D 1 _____   **E** 6 _____

2 _____   7 _____

3 _____   8 _____

4 _____   9 _____

5 _____   10 _____

Number Correct [   ]

Record Page

Name _____   Date _____

Power Builder Color _____   Power Builder Number _____

A Comprehension

1 _____   2 _____   3 _____   4 _____   5 _____

Number Correct [   ]

B, C Learn about Words

1 _____   6 _____

2 _____   7 _____

3 _____   8 _____

4 _____   9 _____

5 _____   10 _____

Number Correct [   ]

Think about It

D 1 _____   E 6 _____

2 _____   7 _____

3 _____   8 _____

4 _____   9 _____

5 _____   10 _____

Number Correct [   ]

Record Page

Name _____   Date _____

Power Builder Color _____   Power Builder Number _____

A Comprehension

1 _____   2 _____   3 _____   4 _____   5 _____

Number Correct [   ]

B, C Learn about Words

1 _____   6 _____

2 _____   7 _____

3 _____   8 _____

4 _____   9 _____

5 _____   10 _____

Number Correct [   ]

Think about It

D 1 _____   E 6 _____

2 _____   7 _____

3 _____   8 _____

4 _____   9 _____

5 _____   10 _____

Number Correct [   ]

Record Page

Name _____ Date _____

Power Builder Color _____ Power Builder Number _____

A Comprehension

1 _____ 2 _____ 3 _____ 4 _____ 5 _____

Number Correct [____]

B, C Learn about Words

1 _____ 6 _____

2 _____ 7 _____

3 _____ 8 _____

4 _____ 9 _____

5 _____ 10 _____

Number Correct [____]

Think about It

D 1 _____ **E** 6 _____

2 _____ 7 _____

3 _____ 8 _____

4 _____ 9 _____

5 _____ 10 _____

Number Correct [____]

Record Page

Name _____

Date _____

Power Builder Color _____

Power Builder Number _____

A Comprehension

1 _____ 2 _____ 3 _____ 4 _____ 5 _____

Number Correct [ ]

B, C Learn about Words

1 _____ 6 _____

2 _____ 7 _____

3 _____ 8 _____

4 _____ 9 _____

5 _____ 10 _____

Number Correct [ ]

Think about It

D 1 _____ **E** 6 _____

2 _____ 7 _____

3 _____ 8 _____

4 _____ 9 _____

5 _____ 10 _____

Number Correct [ ]

Record Page

Name _____ Date _____

Power Builder Color _____ Power Builder Number _____

A Comprehension

1 _____ 2 _____ 3 _____ 4 _____ 5 _____

Number Correct [ ]

B, C Learn about Words

1 _____ 6 _____

2 _____ 7 _____

3 _____ 8 _____

4 _____ 9 _____

5 _____ 10 _____

Number Correct [ ]

Think about It

D 1 _____ **E** 6 _____

2 _____ 7 _____

3 _____ 8 _____

4 _____ 9 _____

5 _____ 10 _____

Number Correct [ ]

Record Page

Name _____ Date _____

Power Builder Color _____ Power Builder Number _____

A Comprehension

1 _____ 2 _____ 3 _____ 4 _____ 5 _____

Number Correct ☐

B, C Learn about Words

1 _____ 6 _____

2 _____ 7 _____

3 _____ 8 _____

4 _____ 9 _____

5 _____ 10 _____

Number Correct ☐

Think about It

D 1 _____ **E** 6 _____

2 _____ 7 _____

3 _____ 8 _____

4 _____ 9 _____

5 _____ 10 _____

Number Correct ☐

Record Page

Name _____ Date _____

Power Builder Color _____ Power Builder Number _____

A Comprehension

1 _____ 2 _____ 3 _____ 4 _____ 5 _____

Number Correct [ ]

B, C Learn about Words

1 _____   6 _____

2 _____   7 _____

3 _____   8 _____

4 _____   9 _____

5 _____   10 _____

Number Correct [ ]

Think about It

D 1 _____   E 6 _____

2 _____   7 _____

3 _____   8 _____

4 _____   9 _____

5 _____   10 _____

Number Correct [ ]

Record Page

Name _____   Date _____

Power Builder Color _____   Power Builder Number _____

A Comprehension

1 _____ 2 _____ 3 _____ 4 _____ 5 _____

Number Correct [ ]

B, C Learn about Words

1 _____   6 _____

2 _____   7 _____

3 _____   8 _____

4 _____   9 _____

5 _____   10 _____

Number Correct [ ]

Think about It

D 1 _____   **E** 6 _____

2 _____   7 _____

3 _____   8 _____

4 _____   9 _____

5 _____   10 _____

Number Correct [ ]

Record Page

Name _____   Date _____

Power Builder Color _____   Power Builder Number _____

A Comprehension

1 _____   2 _____   3 _____   4 _____   5 _____

Number Correct [   ]

B, C Learn about Words

1 _____   6 _____

2 _____   7 _____

3 _____   8 _____

4 _____   9 _____

5 _____   10 _____

Number Correct [   ]

Think about It

D 1 _____   **E** 6 _____

2 _____   7 _____

3 _____   8 _____

4 _____   9 _____

5 _____   10 _____

Number Correct [   ]

Record Page

Name _____ Date _____

Power Builder Color _____ Power Builder Number _____

A Comprehension

1 _____ 2 _____ 3 _____ 4 _____ 5 _____

Number Correct [ ]

B, C Learn about Words

1 _____ 6 _____

2 _____ 7 _____

3 _____ 8 _____

4 _____ 9 _____

5 _____ 10 _____

Number Correct [ ]

Think about It

D1 _____ **E**6 _____

2 _____ 7 _____

3 _____ 8 _____

4 _____ 9 _____

5 _____ 10 _____

Number Correct [ ]

Record Page

Name _____ Date _____

Power Builder Color _____ Power Builder Number _____

A Comprehension

1 _____ 2 _____ 3 _____ 4 _____ 5 _____

Number Correct [ ]

B, C Learn about Words

1 _____ 6 _____

2 _____ 7 _____

3 _____ 8 _____

4 _____ 9 _____

5 _____ 10 _____

Number Correct [ ]

Think about It

D 1 _____ **E** 6 _____

2 _____ 7 _____

3 _____ 8 _____

4 _____ 9 _____

5 _____ 10 _____

Number Correct [ ]

Record Page

Name _____ Date _____

Power Builder Color _____ Power Builder Number _____

A Comprehension

1 _____ 2 _____ 3 _____ 4 _____ 5 _____

Number Correct [   ]

B, C Learn about Words

1 _____   6 _____

2 _____   7 _____

3 _____   8 _____

4 _____   9 _____

5 _____   10 _____

Number Correct [   ]

Think about It

D 1 _____   **E** 6 _____

2 _____   7 _____

3 _____   8 _____

4 _____   9 _____

5 _____   10 _____

Number Correct [   ]

Record Page

Name _____ Date _____

Power Builder Color _____ Power Builder Number _____

A Comprehension

1 _____ 2 _____ 3 _____ 4 _____ 5 _____

Number Correct [ ]

B, C Learn about Words

1 _____ 6 _____

2 _____ 7 _____

3 _____ 8 _____

4 _____ 9 _____

5 _____ 10 _____

Number Correct [ ]

Think about It

D 1 _____ **E** 6 _____

2 _____ 7 _____

3 _____ 8 _____

4 _____ 9 _____

5 _____ 10 _____

Number Correct [ ]

Record Page

Name _____ Date _____

Power Builder Color _____ Power Builder Number _____

A Comprehension

1 _____ 2 _____ 3 _____ 4 _____ 5 _____

Number Correct [ ]

B, C Learn about Words

1 _____ 6 _____

2 _____ 7 _____

3 _____ 8 _____

4 _____ 9 _____

5 _____ 10 _____

Number Correct [ ]

Think about It

D 1 _____ **E** 6 _____

2 _____ 7 _____

3 _____ 8 _____

4 _____ 9 _____

5 _____ 10 _____

Number Correct [ ]

Record Page

Name _____ Date _____

Power Builder Color _____ Power Builder Number _____

A Comprehension

1 _____ 2 _____ 3 _____ 4 _____ 5 _____

Number Correct ☐

B, C Learn about Words

1 _____ 6 _____

2 _____ 7 _____

3 _____ 8 _____

4 _____ 9 _____

5 _____ 10 _____

Number Correct ☐

Think about It

D1 _____ **E**6 _____

2 _____ 7 _____

3 _____ 8 _____

4 _____ 9 _____

5 _____ 10 _____

Number Correct ☐

Record Page

Name _____ Date _____

Power Builder Color _____ Power Builder Number _____

A Comprehension

1 _____ 2 _____ 3 _____ 4 _____ 5 _____

Number Correct [____]

B, C Learn about Words

1 _____ 6 _____

2 _____ 7 _____

3 _____ 8 _____

4 _____ 9 _____

5 _____ 10 _____

Number Correct [____]

Think about It

D 1 _____ **E** 6 _____

2 _____ 7 _____

3 _____ 8 _____

4 _____ 9 _____

5 _____ 10 _____

Number Correct [____]

Record Page

Name _____ Date _____

Power Builder Color _____ Power Builder Number _____

A Comprehension

1 _____ 2 _____ 3 _____ 4 _____ 5 _____

Number Correct ☐

B, C Learn about Words

1 _____ 6 _____

2 _____ 7 _____

3 _____ 8 _____

4 _____ 9 _____

5 _____ 10 _____

Number Correct ☐

Think about It

D 1 _____ **E** 6 _____

2 _____ 7 _____

3 _____ 8 _____

4 _____ 9 _____

5 _____ 10 _____

Number Correct ☐

Record Page

Name _____ Date _____

Power Builder Color _____ Power Builder Number _____

A Comprehension

1 _____ 2 _____ 3 _____ 4 _____ 5 _____

Number Correct [ ]

B, C Learn about Words

1 _____ 6 _____

2 _____ 7 _____

3 _____ 8 _____

4 _____ 9 _____

5 _____ 10 _____

Number Correct [ ]

Think about It

D 1 _____ **E** 6 _____

2 _____ 7 _____

3 _____ 8 _____

4 _____ 9 _____

5 _____ 10 _____

Number Correct [ ]

Record Page

Name _____ Date _____

Power Builder Color _____ Power Builder Number _____

A Comprehension

1 _____ 2 _____ 3 _____ 4 _____ 5 _____

Number Correct [   ]

B, C Learn about Words

1 _____ 6 _____

2 _____ 7 _____

3 _____ 8 _____

4 _____ 9 _____

5 _____ 10 _____

Number Correct [   ]

Think about It

D 1 _____ **E** 6 _____

2 _____ 7 _____

3 _____ 8 _____

4 _____ 9 _____

5 _____ 10 _____

Number Correct [   ]

Record Page

Name _____ Date _____

Power Builder Color _____ Power Builder Number _____

A Comprehension

1 _____ 2 _____ 3 _____ 4 _____ 5 _____

Number Correct [　]

B, C Learn about Words

1 _____ 6 _____

2 _____ 7 _____

3 _____ 8 _____

4 _____ 9 _____

5 _____ 10 _____

Number Correct [　]

Think about It

D 1 _____ **E** 6 _____

2 _____ 7 _____

3 _____ 8 _____

4 _____ 9 _____

5 _____ 10 _____

Number Correct [　]

Record Page

Name _____ Date _____

Power Builder Color _____ Power Builder Number _____

A Comprehension

1 _____ 2 _____ 3 _____ 4 _____ 5 _____

Number Correct [____]

B, C Learn about Words

1 _____ 6 _____

2 _____ 7 _____

3 _____ 8 _____

4 _____ 9 _____

5 _____ 10 _____

Number Correct [____]

Think about It

D 1 _____ E 6 _____

2 _____ 7 _____

3 _____ 8 _____

4 _____ 9 _____

5 _____ 10 _____

Number Correct [____]

Record Page

Name _____ Date _____

Power Builder Color _____ Power Builder Number _____

A Comprehension

1 _____ 2 _____ 3 _____ 4 _____ 5 _____

Number Correct ☐

B, C Learn about Words

1 _____ 6 _____

2 _____ 7 _____

3 _____ 8 _____

4 _____ 9 _____

5 _____ 10 _____

Number Correct ☐

Think about It

D 1 _____ **E** 6 _____

2 _____ 7 _____

3 _____ 8 _____

4 _____ 9 _____

5 _____ 10 _____

Number Correct ☐

Record Page

Name _____   Date _____

Power Builder Color _____   Power Builder Number _____

A   Comprehension

1 _____   2 _____   3 _____   4 _____   5 _____

Number Correct [   ]

B, C   Learn about Words

1 _____   6 _____

2 _____   7 _____

3 _____   8 _____

4 _____   9 _____

5 _____   10 _____

Number Correct [   ]

Think about It

D1 _____   E6 _____

2 _____   7 _____

3 _____   8 _____

4 _____   9 _____

5 _____   10 _____

Number Correct [   ]

Record Page

Name _____ Date _____

Power Builder Color _____ Power Builder Number _____

A Comprehension

1 _____ 2 _____ 3 _____ 4 _____ 5 _____

Number Correct [ ]

B, C Learn about Words

1 _____ 6 _____

2 _____ 7 _____

3 _____ 8 _____

4 _____ 9 _____

5 _____ 10 _____

Number Correct [ ]

Think about It

D1 _____ E6 _____

2 _____ 7 _____

3 _____ 8 _____

4 _____ 9 _____

5 _____ 10 _____

Number Correct [ ]

Record Page

Name _____   Date _____

Power Builder Color _____   Power Builder Number _____

A Comprehension

1 _____   2 _____   3 _____   4 _____   5 _____

Number Correct [ ]

B, C Learn about Words

1 _____   6 _____

2 _____   7 _____

3 _____   8 _____

4 _____   9 _____

5 _____   10 _____

Number Correct [ ]

Think about It

D 1 _____   **E** 6 _____

2 _____   7 _____

3 _____   8 _____

4 _____   9 _____

5 _____   10 _____

Number Correct [ ]

Record Page

Name _____ Date _____

Power Builder Color _____ Power Builder Number _____

A Comprehension

1 _____ 2 _____ 3 _____ 4 _____ 5 _____

Number Correct ☐

B, C Learn about Words

1 _____ 6 _____

2 _____ 7 _____

3 _____ 8 _____

4 _____ 9 _____

5 _____ 10 _____

Number Correct ☐

Think about It

D 1 _____ E 6 _____

2 _____ 7 _____

3 _____ 8 _____

4 _____ 9 _____

5 _____ 10 _____

Number Correct ☐

Record Page

Name _____

Date _____

Power Builder Color _____

Power Builder Number _____

A Comprehension

1 _____ 2 _____ 3 _____ 4 _____ 5 _____

Number Correct ☐

B, C Learn about Words

1 _____ 6 _____

2 _____ 7 _____

3 _____ 8 _____

4 _____ 9 _____

5 _____ 10 _____

Number Correct ☐

Think about It

D 1 _____ **E** 6 _____

2 _____ 7 _____

3 _____ 8 _____

4 _____ 9 _____

5 _____ 10 _____

Number Correct ☐

Record Page

Name _____   Date _____

Power Builder Color _____   Power Builder Number _____

A Comprehension

1 _____ 2 _____ 3 _____ 4 _____ 5 _____

Number Correct [   ]

B, C Learn about Words

1 _____   6 _____

2 _____   7 _____

3 _____   8 _____

4 _____   9 _____

5 _____   10 _____

Number Correct [   ]

Think about It

D1 _____   E6 _____

2 _____   7 _____

3 _____   8 _____

4 _____   9 _____

5 _____   10 _____

Number Correct [   ]

Record Page

Name _____ Date _____

Power Builder Color _____ Power Builder Number _____

A Comprehension

1 _____ 2 _____ 3 _____ 4 _____ 5 _____

Number Correct [ ]

B, C Learn about Words

1 _____ 6 _____

2 _____ 7 _____

3 _____ 8 _____

4 _____ 9 _____

5 _____ 10 _____

Number Correct [ ]

Think about It

D 1 _____ E 6 _____

2 _____ 7 _____

3 _____ 8 _____

4 _____ 9 _____

5 _____ 10 _____

Number Correct [ ]

Record Page

Name _____ Date _____

Power Builder Color _____ Power Builder Number _____

A Comprehension

1 _____ 2 _____ 3 _____ 4 _____ 5 _____

Number Correct [＿＿]

B, C Learn about Words

1 _____   6 _____

2 _____   7 _____

3 _____   8 _____

4 _____   9 _____

5 _____   10 _____

Number Correct [＿＿]

Think about It

D 1 _____   E 6 _____

2 _____   7 _____

3 _____   8 _____

4 _____   9 _____

5 _____   10 _____

Number Correct [＿＿]

Record Page

Name _____ Date _____

Power Builder Color _____ Power Builder Number _____

A Comprehension

1 _____ 2 _____ 3 _____ 4 _____ 5 _____

Number Correct ☐

B, C Learn about Words

1 _____ 6 _____

2 _____ 7 _____

3 _____ 8 _____

4 _____ 9 _____

5 _____ 10 _____

Number Correct ☐

Think about It

D 1 _____ **E** 6 _____

2 _____ 7 _____

3 _____ 8 _____

4 _____ 9 _____

5 _____ 10 _____

Number Correct ☐

My Reading Progress Chart: PURPLE LEVEL

Power Builder Number	Date

Fill in a box for every correct answer on your Power Builder.

A						B,C							D			
1	2	3	4	5		1	2	3	4	5	6		1	2	3	4
1	2	3	4	5		1	2	3	4	5	6		1	2	3	4
1	2	3	4	5		1	2	3	4	5	6		1	2	3	4
1	2	3	4	5		1	2	3	4	5	6		1	2	3	4
1	2	3	4	5		1	2	3	4	5	6		1	2	3	4
1	2	3	4	5		1	2	3	4	5	6		1	2	3	4
1	2	3	4	5		1	2	3	4	5	6		1	2	3	4
1	2	3	4	5		1	2	3	4	5	6		1	2	3	4
1	2	3	4	5		1	2	3	4	5	6		1	2	3	4
1	2	3	4	5		1	2	3	4	5	6		1	2	3	4
1	2	3	4	5		1	2	3	4	5	6		1	2	3	4
1	2	3	4	5		1	2	3	4	5	6		1	2	3	4

My Reading Progress Chart: VIOLET LEVEL

Fill in a box for every correct answer on your Power Builder.

A

1	2	3	4	5
1	2	3	4	5
1	2	3	4	5
1	2	3	4	5
1	2	3	4	5
1	2	3	4	5
1	2	3	4	5
1	2	3	4	5
1	2	3	4	5
1	2	3	4	5
1	2	3	4	5
1	2	3	4	5

B,C

1	2	3	4	5	6
1	2	3	4	5	6
1	2	3	4	5	6
1	2	3	4	5	6
1	2	3	4	5	6
1	2	3	4	5	6
1	2	3	4	5	6
1	2	3	4	5	6
1	2	3	4	5	6
1	2	3	4	5	6
1	2	3	4	5	6
1	2	3	4	5	6

D

1	2	3	4
1	2	3	4
1	2	3	4
1	2	3	4
1	2	3	4
1	2	3	4
1	2	3	4
1	2	3	4
1	2	3	4
1	2	3	4
1	2	3	4
1	2	3	4

Date

Power Builder Number

My Reading Progress Chart: ROSE LEVEL

Fill in a box for every correct answer on your Power Builder.

Power Builder Number	Date

A Comprehension

1	2	3	4	5
1	2	3	4	5
1	2	3	4	5
1	2	3	4	5
1	2	3	4	5
1	2	3	4	5
1	2	3	4	5
1	2	3	4	5
1	2	3	4	5
1	2	3	4	5
1	2	3	4	5
1	2	3	4	5

B, C Learn about Words

1	2	3	4	5	6
1	2	3	4	5	6
1	2	3	4	5	6
1	2	3	4	5	6
1	2	3	4	5	6
1	2	3	4	5	6
1	2	3	4	5	6
1	2	3	4	5	6
1	2	3	4	5	6
1	2	3	4	5	6
1	2	3	4	5	6

D Think about It

1	2	3	4
1	2	3	4
1	2	3	4
1	2	3	4
1	2	3	4
1	2	3	4
1	2	3	4
1	2	3	4
1	2	3	4
1	2	3	4
1	2	3	4

My Reading Progress Chart: RED LEVEL

Fill in a box for every correct answer on your Power Builder.

A Comprehension

1	2	3	4	5
1	2	3	4	5
1	2	3	4	5
1	2	3	4	5
1	2	3	4	5
1	2	3	4	5
1	2	3	4	5
1	2	3	4	5
1	2	3	4	5
1	2	3	4	5
1	2	3	4	5
1	2	3	4	5
1	2	3	4	5

B,C Learn about Words

1	2	3	4	5	6
1	2	3	4	5	6
1	2	3	4	5	6
1	2	3	4	5	6
1	2	3	4	5	6
1	2	3	4	5	6
1	2	3	4	5	6
1	2	3	4	5	6
1	2	3	4	5	6
1	2	3	4	5	6
1	2	3	4	5	6
1	2	3	4	5	6
1	2	3	4	5	6

D Think about It

1	2	3	4
1	2	3	4
1	2	3	4
1	2	3	4
1	2	3	4
1	2	3	4
1	2	3	4
1	2	3	4
1	2	3	4
1	2	3	4
1	2	3	4
1	2	3	4
1	2	3	4

Power Builder Number	Date

My Reading Progress Chart: ORANGE LEVEL

Fill in a box for every correct answer on your Power Builder.

Power Builder Number	Date	A Comprehension					B,C Learn about Words										D Think about It			
		1	2	3	4	5	1	2	3	4	5	6	7	8	9	10	1	2	3	4
		1	2	3	4	5	1	2	3	4	5	6	7	8	9	10	1	2	3	4
		1	2	3	4	5	1	2	3	4	5	6	7	8	9	10	1	2	3	4
		1	2	3	4	5	1	2	3	4	5	6	7	8	9	10	1	2	3	4
		1	2	3	4	5	1	2	3	4	5	6	7	8	9	10	1	2	3	4
		1	2	3	4	5	1	2	3	4	5	6	7	8	9	10	1	2	3	4
		1	2	3	4	5	1	2	3	4	5	6	7	8	9	10	1	2	3	4
		1	2	3	4	5	1	2	3	4	5	6	7	8	9	10	1	2	3	4
		1	2	3	4	5	1	2	3	4	5	6	7	8	9	10	1	2	3	4
		1	2	3	4	5	1	2	3	4	5	6	7	8	9	10	1	2	3	4
		1	2	3	4	5	1	2	3	4	5	6	7	8	9	10	1	2	3	4
		1	2	3	4	5	1	2	3	4	5	6	7	8	9	10	1	2	3	4

My Reading Progress Chart: GOLD LEVEL

Fill in a box for every correct answer on your Power Builder.

A Comprehension

1	2	3	4	5
1	2	3	4	5
1	2	3	4	5
1	2	3	4	5
1	2	3	4	5
1	2	3	4	5
1	2	3	4	5
1	2	3	4	5
1	2	3	4	5
1	2	3	4	5
1	2	3	4	5
1	2	3	4	5
1	2	3	4	5
1	2	3	4	5
1	2	3	4	5

B,C Learn about Words

1	2	3	4	5	6	7	8	9	10
1	2	3	4	5	6	7	8	9	10
1	2	3	4	5	6	7	8	9	10
1	2	3	4	5	6	7	8	9	10
1	2	3	4	5	6	7	8	9	10
1	2	3	4	5	6	7	8	9	10
1	2	3	4	5	6	7	8	9	10
1	2	3	4	5	6	7	8	9	10
1	2	3	4	5	6	7	8	9	10
1	2	3	4	5	6	7	8	9	10
1	2	3	4	5	6	7	8	9	10
1	2	3	4	5	6	7	8	9	10
1	2	3	4	5	6	7	8	9	10
1	2	3	4	5	6	7	8	9	10
1	2	3	4	5	6	7	8	9	10

D Think about It

1	2	3	4
1	2	3	4
1	2	3	4
1	2	3	4
1	2	3	4
1	2	3	4
1	2	3	4
1	2	3	4
1	2	3	4
1	2	3	4
1	2	3	4
1	2	3	4
1	2	3	4
1	2	3	4
1	2	3	4

Power Builder Number	Date

My Reading Progress Chart: BROWN LEVEL

Fill in a box for every correct answer on your Power Builder.

Power Builder Number											
Date											

A Comprehension

Each row: 1 2 3 4 5

1	2	3	4	5
1	2	3	4	5
1	2	3	4	5
1	2	3	4	5
1	2	3	4	5
1	2	3	4	5
1	2	3	4	5
1	2	3	4	5
1	2	3	4	5
1	2	3	4	5
1	2	3	4	5
1	2	3	4	5

B,C Learn about Words

Each row: 1 2 3 4 5 6 7 8 9 10

1	2	3	4	5	6	7	8	9	10
1	2	3	4	5	6	7	8	9	10
1	2	3	4	5	6	7	8	9	10
1	2	3	4	5	6	7	8	9	10
1	2	3	4	5	6	7	8	9	10
1	2	3	4	5	6	7	8	9	10
1	2	3	4	5	6	7	8	9	10
1	2	3	4	5	6	7	8	9	10
1	2	3	4	5	6	7	8	9	10
1	2	3	4	5	6	7	8	9	10
1	2	3	4	5	6	7	8	9	10
1	2	3	4	5	6	7	8	9	10

D Think about It

Each row: 1 2 3 4 5

1	2	3	4	5
1	2	3	4	5
1	2	3	4	5
1	2	3	4	5
1	2	3	4	5
1	2	3	4	5
1	2	3	4	5
1	2	3	4	5
1	2	3	4	5
1	2	3	4	5
1	2	3	4	5

My Reading Progress Chart: TAN LEVEL

Fill in a box for every correct answer on your Power Builder.

A Comprehension

Power Builder Number	Date	A Comprehension	B,C Learn about Words	D Think about It
		1 2 3 4 5	1 2 3 4 5 6 7 8 9 10	1 2 3 4 5
		1 2 3 4 5	1 2 3 4 5 6 7 8 9 10	1 2 3 4 5
		1 2 3 4 5	1 2 3 4 5 6 7 8 9 10	1 2 3 4 5
		1 2 3 4 5	1 2 3 4 5 6 7 8 9 10	1 2 3 4 5
		1 2 3 4 5	1 2 3 4 5 6 7 8 9 10	1 2 3 4 5
		1 2 3 4 5	1 2 3 4 5 6 7 8 9 10	1 2 3 4 5
		1 2 3 4 5	1 2 3 4 5 6 7 8 9 10	1 2 3 4 5
		1 2 3 4 5	1 2 3 4 5 6 7 8 9 10	1 2 3 4 5
		1 2 3 4 5	1 2 3 4 5 6 7 8 9 10	1 2 3 4 5
		1 2 3 4 5	1 2 3 4 5 6 7 8 9 10	1 2 3 4 5
		1 2 3 4 5	1 2 3 4 5 6 7 8 9 10	1 2 3 4 5
		1 2 3 4 5	1 2 3 4 5 6 7 8 9 10	1 2 3 4 5

My Reading Progress Chart: LIME LEVEL

Fill in a box for every correct answer on your Power Builder.

Power Builder Number	Date

A Comprehension

1	2	3	4	5

B,C Learn about Words

1	2	3	4	5	6	7	8	9	10

D Think about It

1	2	3	4	5

My Reading Progress Chart: GREEN LEVEL

Fill in a box for every correct answer on your Power Builder.

Power Builder Number	Date	A Comprehension	B,C Learn about Words	D Think about It
		1 2 3 4 5	1 2 3 4 5 6 7 8 9 10	1 2 3 4 5
		1 2 3 4 5	1 2 3 4 5 6 7 8 9 10	1 2 3 4 5
		1 2 3 4 5	1 2 3 4 5 6 7 8 9 10	1 2 3 4 5
		1 2 3 4 5	1 2 3 4 5 6 7 8 9 10	1 2 3 4 5
		1 2 3 4 5	1 2 3 4 5 6 7 8 9 10	1 2 3 4 5
		1 2 3 4 5	1 2 3 4 5 6 7 8 9 10	1 2 3 4 5
		1 2 3 4 5	1 2 3 4 5 6 7 8 9 10	1 2 3 4 5
		1 2 3 4 5	1 2 3 4 5 6 7 8 9 10	1 2 3 4 5
		1 2 3 4 5	1 2 3 4 5 6 7 8 9 10	1 2 3 4 5
		1 2 3 4 5	1 2 3 4 5 6 7 8 9 10	1 2 3 4 5
		1 2 3 4 5	1 2 3 4 5 6 7 8 9 10	1 2 3 4 5
		1 2 3 4 5	1 2 3 4 5 6 7 8 9 10	1 2 3 4 5

My Reading Progress Chart: AQUA LEVEL

Fill in a box for every correct answer on your Power Builder.

Power Builder Number	Date	A Comprehension					B,C Learn about Words										D, E Think about It									
		1	2	3	4	5	1	2	3	4	5	6	7	8	9	10	1	2	3	4	5	6	7	8	9	10
		1	2	3	4	5	1	2	3	4	5	6	7	8	9	10	1	2	3	4	5	6	7	8	9	10
		1	2	3	4	5	1	2	3	4	5	6	7	8	9	10	1	2	3	4	5	6	7	8	9	10
		1	2	3	4	5	1	2	3	4	5	6	7	8	9	10	1	2	3	4	5	6	7	8	9	10
		1	2	3	4	5	1	2	3	4	5	6	7	8	9	10	1	2	3	4	5	6	7	8	9	10
		1	2	3	4	5	1	2	3	4	5	6	7	8	9	10	1	2	3	4	5	6	7	8	9	10
		1	2	3	4	5	1	2	3	4	5	6	7	8	9	10	1	2	3	4	5	6	7	8	9	10
		1	2	3	4	5	1	2	3	4	5	6	7	8	9	10	1	2	3	4	5	6	7	8	9	10
		1	2	3	4	5	1	2	3	4	5	6	7	8	9	10	1	2	3	4	5	6	7	8	9	10
		1	2	3	4	5	1	2	3	4	5	6	7	8	9	10	1	2	3	4	5	6	7	8	9	10
		1	2	3	4	5	1	2	3	4	5	6	7	8	9	10	1	2	3	4	5	6	7	8	9	10
		1	2	3	4	5	1	2	3	4	5	6	7	8	9	10	1	2	3	4	5	6	7	8	9	10

My Reading Progress Chart: BLUE LEVEL

Fill in a box for every correct answer on your Power Builder.

Power Builder Number	Date	A Comprehension	B,C Learn about Words	D,E Think about It
		1 2 3 4 5	1 2 3 4 5 6 7 8 9 10	1 2 3 4 5 6 7 8 9 10
		1 2 3 4 5	1 2 3 4 5 6 7 8 9 10	1 2 3 4 5 6 7 8 9 10
		1 2 3 4 5	1 2 3 4 5 6 7 8 9 10	1 2 3 4 5 6 7 8 9 10
		1 2 3 4 5	1 2 3 4 5 6 7 8 9 10	1 2 3 4 5 6 7 8 9 10
		1 2 3 4 5	1 2 3 4 5 6 7 8 9 10	1 2 3 4 5 6 7 8 9 10
		1 2 3 4 5	1 2 3 4 5 6 7 8 9 10	1 2 3 4 5 6 7 8 9 10
		1 2 3 4 5	1 2 3 4 5 6 7 8 9 10	1 2 3 4 5 6 7 8 9 10
		1 2 3 4 5	1 2 3 4 5 6 7 8 9 10	1 2 3 4 5 6 7 8 9 10
		1 2 3 4 5	1 2 3 4 5 6 7 8 9 10	1 2 3 4 5 6 7 8 9 10
		1 2 3 4 5	1 2 3 4 5 6 7 8 9 10	1 2 3 4 5 6 7 8 9 10
		1 2 3 4 5	1 2 3 4 5 6 7 8 9 10	1 2 3 4 5 6 7 8 9 10
		1 2 3 4 5	1 2 3 4 5 6 7 8 9 10	1 2 3 4 5 6 7 8 9 10
		1 2 3 4 5	1 2 3 4 5 6 7 8 9 10	1 2 3 4 5 6 7 8 9 10
		1 2 3 4 5	1 2 3 4 5 6 7 8 9 10	1 2 3 4 5 6 7 8 9 10

Answer Keys

Starter 1–Rose

Comprehension
A 1 a
  2 b
  3 b
  4 a
  5 a

Learn about Words
B 1 bad
  2 had
  3 dad

C 4 bad
  5 dad
  6 had

Think about It
D 1 cold
  2 soft
  3 short
  4 down

Starter 2–Rose

Comprehension
A 1 b
  2 b
  3 a
  4 a
  5 b

Learn about Words
B 1 let
  2 pet
  3 get

C 4 pet
  5 let
  6 get

Think about It
D 1 shop
  2 small
  3 hat
  4 glad

Starter 3–Rose

Comprehension
A 1 b
  2 a
  3 b
  4 a
  5 a

Learn about Words
B 1 day
  2 may
  3 way

C 4 way
  5 may
  6 day

Think about It
D 1 yes
  2 no
  3 yes
  4 yes

Starter 4–Red

Comprehension
A 1 a
  2 a
  3 a
  4 b
  5 b

Learn about Words
B 1 can
  2 man
  3 ran

C 4 man
  5 can
  6 ran

Think about It
D 1 begin
  2 last
  3 dad
  4 face

Starter 5–Orange

Comprehension
A 1 b
  2 a
  3 a
  4 a
  5 b

Learn about Words
B 1 pay
  2 may
  3 play
  4 stay
  5 tray

C 6 play
  7 tray
  8 pay
  9 stay
  10 may

Think about It
D 1 a
  2 b
  3 b
  4 a

Starter 6–Gold

Comprehension
A 1 a
  2 b
  3 a
  4 b
  5 b

Learn about Words
B 1 call
  2 fall
  3 tall
  4 small
  5 wall

C 6 tall
  7 small
  8 fall
  9 call
  10 wall

Think about It
D 1 class
  2 big
  3 daddy
  4 space

Strategy Lesson 2
  1 b   3 a
  2 a   4 a